NEW VANGUARD • 166

BRITISH MOTOR GUN BOAT 1939–45

ANGUS KONSTAM   ILLUSTRATED BY TONY BRYAN

First published in Great Britain in 2010 by Osprey Publishing,
Midland House, West Way, Botley, Oxford, OX2 0PH, UK
44–02 23rd St, Suite 219, Long Island City, NY 11101, USA
E-mail: info@ospreypublishing.com

© 2010 Osprey Publishing Ltd.

A CIP catalogue record for this book is available from the British Library

Print ISBN: 978 1 84908 077 4
PDF e-book ISBN: 978 1 84908 078 1

Page layout by: Melissa Orrom Swan, Oxford
Index by Mike Parkin
Typeset in Sabon and Myriad Pro
Originated by PDQ Media, Bungay, UK
Printed in China through Worldprint Ltd

10 11 12 13 14   10 9 8 7 6 5 4 3 2 1

AUTHOR'S NOTE

All photographs are from the Stratford Archive, unless noted otherwise.

ABBREVIATIONS

BPB – British Power Boat Company
LMG – light machine gun
M/L – motor launch
MA/SB – motor anti-submarine boats
MG – machine gun
MGB – motor gun boat
MTB – motor torpedo boat
PT – patrol torpedo (patrol boat)
PTC – patrol torpedo craft (motor boat submarine chaser)
SGB – Steam Gun Boats
SOE – Special Operations Executive

FOR A CATALOGUE OF ALL BOOKS PUBLISHED BY OSPREY MILITARY
AND AVIATION PLEASE CONTACT:

NORTH AMERICA
Osprey Direct, c/o Random House Distribution Center,
400 Hahn Road, Westminster, MD 21157
E-mail: uscustomerservice@ospreypublishing.com

ALL OTHER REGIONS
Osprey Direct, The Book Service Ltd, Distribution Centre,
Colchester Road, Frating Green, Colchester, Essex, CO7 7DW
E-mail: customerservice@ospreypublishing.com

Osprey Publishing is supporting the Woodland Trust, the UK's
leading woodland conservation charity, by funding the dedication
of trees.

www.ospreypublishing.com

CONTENTS

BRITISH MOTOR GUN BOAT 1939–45

INTRODUCTION

When Britain entered World War II, the Royal Navy might have been the most powerful fleet in the world, but it was woefully short of small boats – the craft Britain needed to protect its coastal convoys or to attack enemy coastal shipping. These small boats, the craft of 'Coastal Forces', played a vital part in vying for control of the sea lanes, both in home waters and further afield. Apart from a handful of motor torpedo boats (MTBs), the Navy lacked the vessels it needed to fight this crucial campaign.

The development, appearance and operation of these MTBs has been covered in an earlier book in this series: *British Motor Torpedo Boat, 1939–45* (Osprey New Vanguard 74). However glamorous these little boats might appear, they were only part of the story. MTBs have been described as bombers, flying towards their targets to deliver their payload. By contrast, motor gun boats (MGBs) have been seen as the fighters, swooping in to engage and destroy the enemy's fighters and bombers. Even more romantically, MGBs have been described – with some justification – as the 'Spitfires of the Seas'.

The Fairmile D was the ultimate development of the MGB. Although most of these vessels were fitted with torpedoes, like many of the 'Dog Boats' serving in the Mediterranean, MGB-663 remained a thoroughbred MGB throughout the war.

In fact, the story of MGBs is a lot more complex, as is the role they played in the battles fought by British Coastal Forces during World War II. For a start, they were designed as an afterthought, once the war had already started. It was discovered that the lightly armed MTBs were unable to match German E-Boats in firepower, so they needed some form of protection. At first, MGBs were converted from existing small warships, but eventually purpose-built gun boats began to enter service. By 1943 the powerful Fairmile D class of MGB had joined the fight, although by that time the difference between MGBs and MTBs was becoming blurred. By the end of the war, the Royal Navy possessed some of the best-armed small warships for their size in the world, vessels that were more than a match for their Axis counterparts. This book is their story.

DEVELOPMENT

British Power Boat MGBs

On 3 September 1939 the Royal Navy had no Coastal Forces to speak of. No official organization existed before October 1940, and there were precious few warships in service. While new vessels were being built, all the Royal Navy had in service were a handful of MTBs and five motor anti-submarine boats (MA/SBs). The threat of war in 1938 had resulted in the ordering of new vessels – MTBs from the yards of Vosper, White and Thornycroft, and MA/SBs from the British Power Boat Company (BPB), based in Hythe, in Sussex. Although nobody suspected it at the time, these small craft would form the nucleus of Britain's MGB fleet.

BPB was founded in 1927 by power boat enthusiast Hubert Scott-Paine. He wanted to build boats that would skim over the water rather than slice through it, but which were responsive to handle and manoeuvrable. He designed what were essentially speedboat hulls, and powered his craft with specially developed lightweight engines. During the 1930s he built high-speed launches for the Royal Navy, while his power boat *Miss Great Britain III* won international racing trophies, bringing Scott-Paine and his firm worldwide recognition.

MGB-108, a 71ft 9in BPB MGP, photographed off the Kent coast near Ramsgate in May 1943. Later that summer she was provided with torpedo tubes and redesignated MTB-418.

BPB 70ft MGBs, pictured in 1941 after their conversion from MA/SB boats. The boats are travelling at around 20 knots – at faster speeds the boats produced a highly visible wake, and the stern would be almost completely submerged.

By 1935, the Admiralty was becoming worried that both Germany and Italy were developing high-speed motor boats. Consequently Scott-Paine was commissioned to build a prototype 50ft MTB – the first time the term was used in the Royal Navy. This project proved successful, and in 1937 the Admiralty placed an order for six boats, albeit ones whose length was increased to 60ft. On entering service, these boats formed the 1st MTB Flotilla, which was sent to the Mediterranean for evaluation. By 1937, another dozen 60ft boats had entered service. These were used to form two more MTB flotillas, one of which was sent to Hong Kong, and the other to Malta.

During 1938 Scott-Paine designed an improved version of his MTB, with a 70ft hull and powered by Rolls Royce engines. In early 1939, it seemed that the flamboyant Scott-Paine had antagonized senior figures in the Admiralty and Whitehall, and contracts for new boats were awarded to BPB's rivals, the Vosper Company and Thornycroft Marine. In 1940 a disgusted Scott-Paine sailed to the United States, taking his 70ft prototype with him. The US Navy proved more amenable, and the boat was accepted into service as PT-6, becoming the prototype for the Patrol Torpedo (PT) boats produced by the Elco Company.

Meanwhile, BPB concentrated on building MTBs and MA/SBs for foreign navies. In 1938, however, the Admiralty did issue a contract for a group of five MA/SB boats, which were essentially 60ft BMP MTBs, but carrying depth charges and Asdic (sonar), instead of torpedo tubes. These entered service in early 1939 as MA/SBs 1–5. The order was followed by another in 1939, followed by a second for a larger MA/SB design, based on Scott-Paine's 70ft hull. The motivation behind the MA/SB was that the Admiralty was concerned about German U-Boats operating in British coastal waters, and it decided it needed small coastal submarine-hunting vessels that could patrol harbours, estuaries and coastal shipping lanes. In fact, by 1940 it was clear that the Germans preferred hunting for bigger mercantile targets in the Western Approaches and the North Atlantic, and they used aircraft-dropped mines to harass British coastal shipping.

In September 1939, the first five MA/SBs were operating off the East Coast, and by the end of the year they were joined by the first of the 59 new BPB MA/SBs ordered the previous year, in a second larger contract. The 60ft boats were actually 60ft 3in long, and were powered by two Napier engines, which gave them a top speed of 25 knots. While this performance wasn't highly impressive, it was adequate for the task of submarine hunting in coastal

waters. In fact, Scott-Paine preferred to use more powerful Rolls Royce engines, but by 1939 these had been reserved for use in British aircraft. Just how effective these craft might have been is demonstrated by a group of six 60ft BPB craft, which were being built for foreign navies when the war began. All of these were powered by two Rolls Royce engines, giving the boats a much more impressive top speed of 40 knots. All of them were requisitioned by the Admiralty, and became MA/SBs (and later MGBs) 40–45. Similarly, a group of 13 70ft boats built for the French Navy were powered by three Isotta-Fraschini engines apiece, giving top speeds in excess of 36 knots. These duly became MGBs 50–67.

Another BPB vessel was TMB-51 (Torpedo Motor Boat), which was built for the Royal Netherlands Navy. This 70ft boat was seized by the British in September 1939, but the Dutch crew had already arrived to conduct sea trials – they simply extended the trials as far as the Dutch coast, and TMB-51 duly entered service with the Dutch Navy. In May 1940, however, the Germans overran Holland, and TMB-51's commander sailed her to Britain, where she was converted into an MGB: MGB-46. She was then handed over to a Dutch crew, who formed part of the multi-national 3rd MGB Flotilla.

A 71ft 9in BPB MGB (pennant number unknown), pictured operating at just over half speed. She is armed with a power-mounted 2-pdr in the bow and a twin 20mm Oerlikon in a powered mount in the stern.

MA/SB 22 was one of the 60ft BPB vessels that formed the Coastal Anti-Submarine Flotilla. She is pictured here just after her conversion into MGB-41, in June 1940. The camouflage scheme was light grey and charcoal grey.

By early 1940 it was clear that there was no real need for MA/SBs, but the fall of France in May 1940 gave them a new purpose. With German E-Boats stationed in Dutch, Belgian and French ports, the coastal shipping lanes of the English Channel were threatened, and so the Admiralty decided to convert its fleet of MA/SBs into MGBs. This was the true birth of the British motor gun boat – a makeshift response to the need for small well-armed warships to counter the E-Boat threat. By the end of the summer the majority of BPB MA/SBs had become 60ft and 70ft MGBs, armed with a 2-pdr gun aft, and a pair of twin machine guns (MGs) mounted in turrets on either side of the bridge. A few were retained as MA/SBs – just in case – while others became air-sea rescue launches.

The weakness of the BPB design was its size. The boats were vulnerable due to their highly flammable fuel and their light construction. Even a moderate amount of damage could put them out of action. Therefore, in 1941 BPB began work on a slightly longer and more robust version – a boat just 3in short of 72ft long. These entered service from the late spring of 1942, and both MGB and MTB versions were produced. This time the craft were powered by powerful American Packard supercharged engines, which gave the boats a top speed of 42 knots. They became the mainstay of the British MGB fleet in home waters, at least until the arrival of the more powerful 'Dog Boats' (see below).

The range of the new vessels meant they could operate anywhere along the Dutch, Belgian or French Channel coast, and their powerful armament made them formidable adversaries. The 71ft 9in BPB design proved perfect for Coastal Forces operations, although their crews still complained that they were cramped, and that living conditions were spartan. Some 32 of these MGBs entered service during 1942, and by the end of the war a total of 77 MGBs of this class had been completed, making them the most numerous type of dedicated MGB in service.

Lend-Lease MGBs

In March 1941, President Roosevelt signed the Lend-Lease Act, whereby the United States agreed to supply Britain with war material, including warships, weaponry and funds. A precedent had already been set in 1940, when Roosevelt agreed to transfer 50 obsolete US Navy destroyers to the Royal Navy – a vital stopgap that allowed Britain to protect its transatlantic sea lanes during the darkest period of the Battle of the Atlantic.

BRITISH POWER BOAT MGBS

70ft BPB MGB (above)
The British Power Boat Company of Hythe in Sussex designed the Royal Navy's first dedicated MGBs, and these proved extremely successful. A total of 44 of the 70ft boats were built by the company, powered by a variety of engines and fitted with a range of weaponry. MGB-8 pictured here was relatively lightly armed with a Rolls Royce 2-pdr gun in the stern, and two twin .5in MGs in tub mountings on either side of the bridge.

71ft 9in BPB MGB (below)
This BPB design was introduced in 1942, and used one hull design for both an MGB and an MTB variant. The longer hull allowed the boat to carry a larger array of weapons than the earlier BPB design and these boats were also considerably faster than their predecessors. A total of 77 boats of this kind were completed as MGBs, the majority of which served in home waters. MGB-115 (pictured here) carried a 2-pdr 'pom-pom' in the bow, a single 20mm Oerlikon towards the stern and a Holman Projector further aft, although this was later removed. She also carried two twin .303in MGs on each side of the bridge, and a single depth charge on each beam. The single Oerlikon was replaced by a twin version in 1943.

PT-211, a US Navy 78ft Higgins boat, operated alongside the British Coastal Forces in the Mediterranean and was eventually transferred into Royal Navy service along with the rest of the US 15th MTB Flotilla in October 1944. This vessel became MGB-186.

A total of 79 small warships were transferred from the US Navy to the Royal Navy, including 40 craft built by the Electric Boat Company (Elco) of Bayonne, New Jersey, 34 by the Higgins Boat Company of New Orleans, and five more built to US Navy specifications in the Philadelphia Navy Yard. Of these craft, 29 Higgins boats and 12 Elco boats became British MGBs. In a way, the Elco boats had come home. As we have seen, during the late 1930s the US Navy purchased a prototype 70ft boat designed by Hubert Scott-Paine. She became PT-6 and the US Navy were so impressed that in December 1939 they ordered ten more to be built by Elco under licence, which duly became PTs 10–19. These were designed as PT craft, the American equivalent of the MTB.

After further trials, however, the US Navy decided that these 70ft boats were too short to carry American torpedoes, which were longer than their British counterparts. Consequently Elco redesigned the craft, which became the 77ft Elco PT Boat. In addition, another 12 boats were ordered, but these were designated PTCs (motor boat submarine chasers), and numbered PTCs 1–12. Of these only four (PTCs 1–4) entered service with the US Navy, and in the spring of 1941 they were sent down to Key West, Florida, for evaluation. It was found that the small hulls made poor platforms for sonar operation, so the US Navy were left with ten PT Boats and 12 PTCs that weren't much use to them. The Lend-Lease Act offered them a way out. In April 1941, the ten 70ft Elco PT boats were transferred to the Royal Navy as part of the Lend-Lease programme and duly became MTBs 259–268. The 12 PTCs were transferred at the same time, and were designated MGBs 82–93.

What proved unsuitable for the US Navy proved a godsend for their Royal Naval counterparts. The dozen PTCs arrived in Britain just at the same time as the first of the BPB MA/SBs were being converted into MGBs. As both groups of vessels were designed by Scott-Paine, the 70ft Elco boats proved very similar to the 60ft and 70ft BPB vessels that were earmarked to form the backbone of the new MGB flotillas.

The Elco boats were originally armed with two twin .5in MGs in Perspex-covered Dewandre turrets, one on each side of the bridge. They also carried racks for depth charges, two 'Y' guns (depth charge throwers) and fittings for

MGB-89 was one of the 70ft Elco boats supplied by the US Navy to the Royal Navy in April 1941 as a result of part of the Lend-Lease Act. Her original American designation was PTC-8. Unusually, in this picture taken in early 1942 she still retains her American Dewandre MG turrets.

light MGs on each side of the bridge. The depth charges were removed before the transfer. On receipt, the Royal Navy fitted the dozen Elco boats with a single 20mm Oerlikon in the stern, and replaced the MGs with equivalent .5in Vickers weapons. However, a photo of MGB-89 shows her with the American turrets still in place, so at least some of the boats might have retained their Browning MGs and Dewandre turrets for some time after they entered British service.

At the same time as Elco was developing its own 77ft and 80ft variants of the original Scott-Paine design, Higgins Industries was developing its own type of PT boat. In June 1941, the Higgins prototype became PT-70, a 72ft vessel that proved highly successful. Therefore, in December 1941 the US Navy commissioned more Higgins boats, although after evaluating PT-70 it was decided to increase the length of the vessel to 78ft. The first of these 78ft Higgins boats, PT-71, was completed in July 1942.

The first Higgins boat to enter service with the Royal Navy formed part of the initial Lend-Lease shipment. It was an 81ft experimental boat that had been accepted by the US Navy as PT-6 in August 1940 for evaluation. The design proved less successful than other Higgins craft, and it was transferred to the Royal Navy in the early summer of 1941. Higgins Industries also produced a batch of six 70ft boats, which were shipped to Britain as part of Lend-Lease in the late summer of 1941, without having served in the US Navy. After all, the Americans had already rejected the 70ft Elco equivalents as being too small. These craft were based on the original Scott-Paine design, and were originally built for the Finnish Navy. Still, this made them perfectly compatible with the existing 70ft BPB craft, and so they were duly commissioned as MGBs 69–73. In June another shipment of seven 70ft Higgins boats arrived, and these became MGBs 100–106.

In October 1944, the bulk of the Mediterranean-based US MTB Ron 15 (15th PT Boat Flotilla – PTs 201, 203–217) were transferred to Royal Navy service, becoming MGBs 177–192. These Higgins boats proved reliable, and were popular with their crews. The armament of the 70ft Higgins MGBs was similar to that of the 70ft Elco and BPB vessels, while MGB-68 became a training vessel, based at HMS *St Christopher* – the Coastal Forces Training Base at Fort William in Scotland. The more powerful 78ft Higgins MGBs based in the Mediterranean were armed with a combination of .5in MGs and 20mm Oerlikons.

Early Fairmile M/Ls

In early 1939, Noel Macklin, director of the Fairmile Marine Company, approached the Admiralty with the suggestion that they commission a class of prefabricated motor launches (M/Ls). He believed that they would be of great use as coastal escorts, anti-submarine craft and mine warfare vessels. The big advantage of prefabrication was that while Fairmile made the parts, the vessels themselves could be assembled and finished by wood-working companies that had no previous experience in boatbuilding. Macklin's craft, designed by Norman Hart, would be around 110ft long, displace 50–60 tons, and would be powered by three Hall-Scott Defender petrol engines, giving them a top speed of 25 knots. The design of the hull was based on an existing coastal fishery protection vessel, the *Vaila*.

At first the Admiralty turned Macklin down, but he went ahead and built a prototype anyway – a vessel that would become ML-100. With war looming, the Admiralty had a change of heart, and the prototype was ordered in July 1939. When war broke out in September 1939, the Admiralty ordered another 11 vessels of the same type, as well as 13 more of their own design, which would become the Fairmile B class. By the end of the year, Fairmile had effectively become an offshoot of the Admiralty, and the company spent the rest of the war as an official government agency.

ML-100 was completed in May 1940, which was far later than either Macklin or his Admiralty employers had hoped. The delay was due to

FAIRMILE A AND FAIRMILE B M/LS

Fairmile A M/L (above)
These early Fairmile motor launches were the forerunners of the far more numerous Type B group, and prototypes for the later Fairmile MGBs. The design proved less suitable to Coastal Forces operations than that of the later Fairmile boats, so in early 1941 the majority were converted into coastal minelayers, and spent the war making nocturnal forays into the sea lanes off the Dutch, Belgian and French coasts.

The first of these boats, ML-100, entered service in April 1940. She carried a Hotchkiss 3-pdr aft, twin Lewis guns amidships and another single Lewis gun forward, on a pintle mount. She was also fitted with two racks amidships, each carrying six depth charges. As a minelayer (not pictured) her funnel was removed, the 3-pdr was moved onto the bow and a twin .5in MG mount was fitted into its old position. Her depth charges were also replaced by racks containing a total of six or nine mines, depending on their type.

Fairmile B M/L (below)
These boats proved far superior to the original Fairmile A vessels, and were mass-produced in British and Canadian boatyards. They were designed so that the armament could be altered fairly easily, and consequently the weaponry carried on these boats varied considerably. They also fulfilled a range of roles; coastal escorts, makeshift torpedo boats, anti-submarine vessels, minesweepers, minelayers and gun boats.

ML-455 was built in Cockenzie in East Lothian, and entered service in November 1941 under the command of Lt J. S. Price. She was used in a variety of roles, but is pictured here as she looked in mid-1942, when she was used as a minesweeper. She was then armed with a 3-pdr forward, a single 20mm Oerlikon amidships and a twin 20mm Oerlikon aft. Two twin Lewis guns were mounted on either side of her forecastle, just forward of the bridge, although these were later replaced with signal projectors. She also carried 14 depth charges. A shield was later added to her 3-pdr.

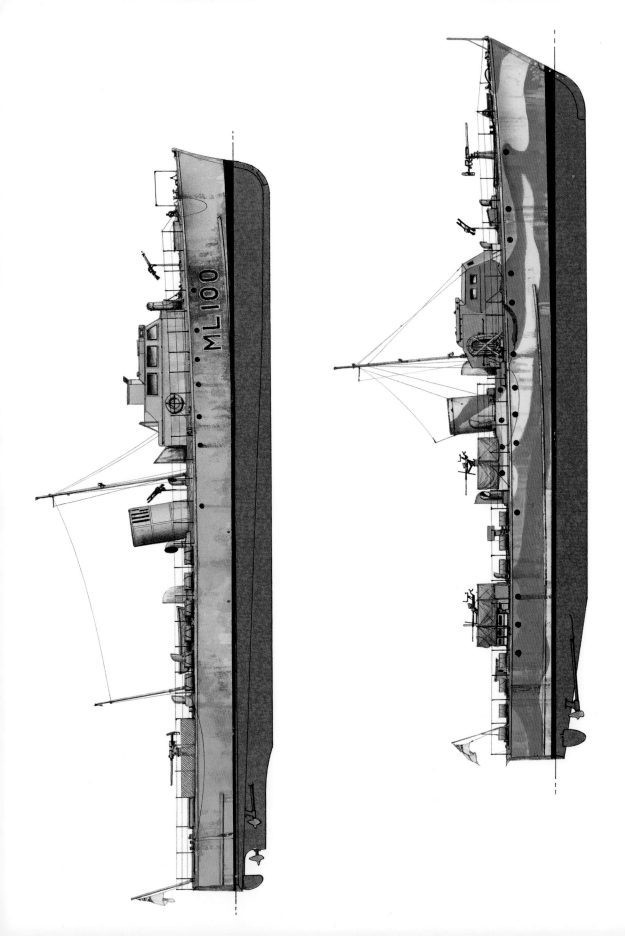

ML-103, a Fairmile A M/L, pictured in the summer of 1941. By that time she had been converted into a minelayer, armed with a 3-pdr (aft), twin Lewis guns, a Holman Projector and two depth charges. Unusually, she still retained her funnel. Her cargo of six ground mines is carried abaft her funnel, three on each beam. (IWM)

modifications to the design of the rudder, designed to improve the vessel's manoeuvring ability at slow speed. In fact, she and the rest of the Fairmile A class remained awkward vessels to handle, and uncomfortable in anything other than calm seas. The prefabricated nature of the design, however, meant that the rest of the vessels could be built quickly, and the remaining 11 Fairmile A vessels were all completed between May and July 1940, in nine different boatyards from the River Clyde to the Isle of Wight.

Strangely enough, the Admiralty ordered the dozen motor launches without first specifying what their armament would be. This meant that their decks weren't specially reinforced to take heavy mountings, and the armament of the motor launches was very much an afterthought. It was decided that this armament would consist of a single 3-pdr aft, supported by single or twin Lewis light machine guns (LMGs). Both weapons were antiquated, but adequate, at least until something better could be fitted in their place. The craft also carried a Holman Projector – an anti-aircraft contraption that fired hand grenades skyward to a height of 600ft. Finally, the Fairmile A M/Ls were capable of carrying a basic form of Asdic, and up to 12 depth charges.

Of course, these vessels were motor launches, not MGBs. Their role was to defend coastal convoys, and to hunt down U-Boats in shallow coastal waters. It was never planned that they would engage in gun duels with enemy warships. However, they provided a vital first step – the prototype of more powerful and better-armed Fairmile boats, which were purpose-built to take

The Fairmile A boat ML-106 was converted into a minelayer in early 1941. In this configuration, her armament consists of a 3-pdr (bow), twin .5in MGs in a central turret mount (aft), a Holman Projector (amidships) and two twin .303in LMGs on either side of the bridge. She also carries six ground mines. (IWM)

ML-117, a Fairmile B Type Motor Launch, was built at Isleworth on the River Thames, and entered service in late October 1940. she formed part of the 2nd ML Flotilla, and was on of the Fairmile boats converted to carry American 21in torpedoes, as part of an anti-invasion measure.

the fight to the enemy. Once the better Fairmile B M/Ls became available after September 1940, the nine surviving Fairmile A vessels were converted into minelayers. Here was a more aggressive role than mere coastal escorts, as it involved venturing across the English Channel into the enemy's coastal shipping lanes. Therefore the craft received an extra twin .5in MG mounted in the stern, while the 3-pdr was moved to the forecastle. By 1943 these weapons were augmented by a single 20mm Oerlikon mounted in place of the funnel, and later still another twin Oerlikon was carried in the stern.

The first Fairmile B M/L was completed in September 1940, and the rest of that original order of 13 boats was completed over the following two months (with the exception of ML-123, which was delayed until the spring of 1941. The Admiralty had such confidence in the Fairmile B design that another 120 boats were ordered in January 1940, and 26 of these entered service before the end of the year. Most of the remainder were completed by the summer of 1941, the product of no fewer than 73 boatyards, with 26 of these located overseas, including yards in Auckland, Cairo, Dar-es-Salaam, Jamaica, Karachi, Rangoon, Sydney and Singapore.

Here was the real beauty of the Fairmile design. Prefabrication meant that the component parts could be shipped around the world, and the boats assembled where they were needed. The Admiralty design itself was a pre-war one, produced by Sydney Graham. The hull shape had been thoroughly tested, and the Admiralty knew it had a successful design. Fairmile then adapted these plans to suit prefabrication, which in turn allowed the boats to be mass produced. A further 97 were ordered in the early summer of 1940, and by the end of World War II no fewer than 650 vessels of the class had been built around the world.

These Fairmile B M/Ls were 112ft long, they displaced 67 tons (although this crept up to 87 tons as more weaponry was added), and they were powered by two Hall-Scott Defenders, giving the vessels a top speed of 20 knots. Like the Fairmile As, these were no gun boats – they were designed to fulfil a variety of less aggressive roles, the most important of which was the escorting of coastal convoys. They were armed with whatever weaponry could be found at the time, including Hotchkiss 3-pdrs, Lewis MGs and more modern Oerlikons. Nine of them were even fitted with a pair of 21in torpedo tubes apiece, taken from old Lend-Lease US destroyers. Despite these craft having a top speed of just 20 knots, these nine vessels of the 2nd ML Flotilla were meant to attack German invasion barges, in the event of an amphibious invasion of Britain. After the threat evaporated, the torpedoes were removed.

In early 1941, nine Fairmile B M/Ls of the 2nd ML Flotilla were fitted with 21in torpedo tubes as an anti-invasion measure. ML-317 and her companions made singularly unsuitable makeshift MTBs, and the tubes were removed later that year.

The Fairmile B M/L soon became the unglamorous backbone of Coastal Forces. These vessels carried out a varied range of roles, being used as coastal escorts, minesweepers, minelayers, navigational leaders (used during Commando raids), anti-submarine craft, patrol boats, rescue launches and ambulance launches. The configurations meant that their armament varied considerably, but a typical well-armed Fairmile B in an escort role during 1941–42 might carry two 3-pdr guns, supported by twin Lewis MGs and depth charges. Later escorts or gun boats were even fitted with 40mm (2-pdr) and 6-pdr guns, and 20mm Oerlikons. While these vessels lacked the speed and glamour of MTBs and MGBs, they helped plug the gap until these MGBs became available. They also acted as a useful prototype, allowing Fairmile and Admiralty designers to develop the Fairmile D – the ultimate British MGB of World War II.

Fairmile C MGBs

While the Fairmile A design had its faults, it proved that the company's prefabricated method of construction could be used to produce finished vessels at great speed. After the fall of France in May 1940, the Royal Navy had a pressing need for escorts and gun boats, hence the conversion of its MA/SB fleet into MGBs. The decision was taken to adapt the Fairmile A design, as the

FAIRMILE C MGB AND DENNY STEAM GUN BOAT

Fairmile C MGB (above)
While this Fairmile design never went into mass production, a total of 24 vessels were produced, and it should be viewed as a forerunner of the highly successful Fairmile D design. In effect, it helped bridge the gap until its larger and more powerful successors were built. Unlike previous Fairmile designs, this was a pure gun boat, and was therefore well armed. MGB-328 was built in Shoreham-by-Sea in Sussex and entered service in November 1941. Her armament was typical of the vessels of this class – a 2-pdr Quick Firing (QF) gun in the bow, a Rolls Royce 2-pdr in the stern, and two twin .5in MGs mounted in tubs amidships, one on each side of the vessel. She was also designed to carry a Holman Projector, but there is no evidence that this was ever shipped. Her powerful armament was augmented by two twin .303in MGs on each bridge wing, and four depth charges mounted amidships, two on each beam. MGB-328 was sunk during an action with German E-Boats in the Dover Straits in July 1942.

Denny SGB (below)
The Denny Steam Gun Boat was the giant of the Coastal Forces fleet, as these vessels were more than 145ft long, which was roughly double the length of most contemporary MGBs or MTBs. They were designed by William Denny and Brothers Ltd. of Dumbarton on the River Clyde, and while a class of 60 were planned, only nine of them were built. These vessels were unusual in that they were given ship names – the vessel pictured here is SGB-9, HMS *Grey Goose*, which was commanded by Lt Cdr Peter Scott, the famous ornithologist. When she first received her name in July 1942 the *Grey Goose* was armed as shown here, with a single 20mm Oerlikon in the bow, a 2-pdr on the forecastle, a 3in HA (high angle) gun in the stern, a Holman Projector amidships, two twin .5in MGs on either side of the bridge and two 21in torpedo tubes. The high pennant number was designed to confuse the unwary, supporting a larger class of boats than there actually was.

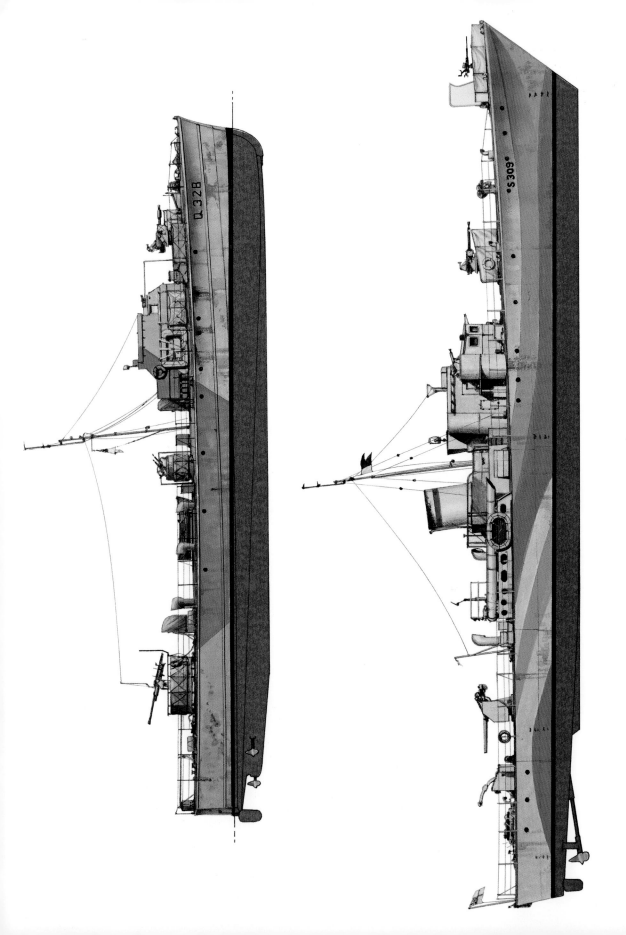

A pair of Fairmile C MGBs, photographed in early 1942. MGB-328 and MGB-330 behind her both carry a powered 2-pdr (bow), a Rolls Royce 2-pdr (stern), two twin .5in MGs in turrets (amidships), two .303in LMGs and four depth charges.

machine tools used to produce its prefabricated parts were still available, which meant production could be started up again with minimal delay.

In late August 1940, the Admiralty commissioned a batch of 24 M/Ls, based on the Fairmile A design but modified to include several important improvements. This new batch of vessels was duly designated the Fairmile C class. Unlike their M/L predecessors, however, these would be powered with three supercharged versions of the Hall-Scott Defender engines fitted in the Fairmile As, which would give the new craft a top speed of around 26½ knots. More importantly, changes to the design of the rudder meant that they were more manoeuvrable, and larger fuel tanks gave them a greater range, allowing Fairmile C MGBs to operate anywhere in the English Channel or its Eastern Approaches. Better still, unlike the smaller BPB MGBs, these – the first long MGBs in British service – were capable of operating in rough seas, which made them far more useful as escorts than their predecessors.

The first Fairmile C was completed in June 1941, and all 24 vessels entered service before the end of the year. For the most part, these boats were used to protect coastal convoys operating in the eastern end of the English Channel, and the Eastern Approaches. However, they also proved suitable for more clandestine work, and the 15th MGB Flotilla, which consisted mainly of Fairmile C vessels, undertook regular cross-Channel missions on behalf of the Special Operations Executive (SOE).

When they first appeared, these MGBs were for the most part armed with a 2-pdr in a powered mounting in the bow, a Rolls Royce 2-pdr in the stern, and two twin turret-mounted .5in MGs amidships. Some also carried a Holman Projector, and two twin .303in Vickers LMGs, one on each side of the bridge. By 1944 the Rolls Royce gun had been replaced by a more efficient second 2-pdr on a power mounting, while most of the MGs were replaced with either single or twin 20mm Oerlikons. Some boats also carried another twin 20mm amidships, in place of the Holman Projector.

The Fairmile C vessel *MGB-326*, photographed leaving Lowestoft harbour in the spring of 1942. The 'Q' prefix was sometimes used as an alternative prefix to 'M/L' or 'MGB'.

Four Fairmile C boats, pictured in Dover harbour in mid-1942. Interestingly, all four boats display minor differences in weaponry and fittings. The two vessels in the foreground are MGBs 324 and 328.

These vessels proved to be reliable, efficient and well armed. While they were originally intended as a stop-gap until the larger Fairmile Ds entered service, they proved so useful that apart from the three boats sunk in action during 1942 (MGBs 314, 328 and 335), and those lost to mines off Normandy in 1944 (MGBs 313 and 326), the remainder stayed in service throughout the war.

Denny Steam Gun Boats (SGBs)

Another slightly more unusual form of MGB was developed by the William Denny Company of Dumbarton, on the River Clyde. In late 1940, the Admiralty approached Denny, who were known as innovators; before the war they were one of the few private firms in Britain to have their own testing tanks. The Admiralty's aim was to produce a long-hulled fast gun boat capable of operating in all weathers, but which had the firepower to deal with enemy E-Boats. In effect, they would be 'super' gun boats. Another Admiralty stipulation was that they would carry a torpedo armament, so that like the powerful German R-Boats (*Raumboote*) they were effectively combined MGB/MTBs. It was also intended that these craft would be prefabricated, allowing them to be constructed quickly and in large numbers.

The result was a 145ft 8in long steel-hulled design, powered by two Metrovick steam turbines, each generating an impressive 4,000hp. The hull was more like that of a miniature destroyer than a conventional Coastal Forces boat, which earned these boats the reputation of being some of the most elegant small warships of World War II. Steel was used for the hull because it could be mass-produced faster than a wooden hull for a vessel of this size. Besides, steel-hulled warships were what Denny did best.

The Admiralty approved the design, although due to a shortage of steel and marine turbines the initial order for 52 vessels was scaled down to just nine. The prefabricated parts were sent to four other small shipyards, while Denny built two vessels themselves (SGB-7 and SGB-8). All these hulls were laid down in early 1941, but the two boats (SGB-1 and SGB-2) being built by

The Denny Steam Gun Boat *Grey Goose* (SGB-9) pictured cruising at speed in the English Channel during the late summer of 1942.

Thornycroft outside Southampton were cancelled, after the hulls were badly damaged in an air raid. Six of the seven remaining Steam Gun Boats were launched before the end of the year, and SGB-9 followed them into the water in February 1942.

All seven gun boats were commissioned before the summer of 1942, and they first saw action in July, when SGB-7 was sunk in action. As a result of this, extra armour was fitted to protect the vulnerable steam boilers, and the modified vessels performed with distinction during the Dieppe Raid in August 1942. By that time, Lt Cdr Peter Scott, commanding SGB-9, had been given permission to name the six remaining vessels, and so SGBs 3–6 and 8–9 became *Grey Seal*, *Grey Fox*, *Grey Owl*, *Grey Shark*, *Grey Wolf* and *Grey Goose* respectively. Generally, the Denny SGBs performed extremely well during the war. Their biggest handicap, however, after the vulnerability of their engines was dealt with, was their size, which made them more conspicuous than other Coastal Forces craft. Of course, it also allowed them to carry a formidable array of weaponry, making them some of the best-armed small vessels of the war.

Fairmile D MGBs

When the British first encountered the German E-Boat, they were thoroughly impressed. The Germans called these small warships S-Boats (from the word *Schnellboot* – 'fast boat'), but the British referred to them as E-Boats, where the

A view forward from the bridge of *Grey Wolf* (SGB-8), showing her gun crews manning her guns – a powered 2-pdr in the foreground and a single 20mm Oerlikon in the bow.

'E' stood for 'Enemy'. They were better armed than British MTBs and short-hulled MGBs, and until mid-1942 only the Fairmile C MGBs and the Denny SGBs could match them in terms of firepower. These German craft were also excellent weapons platforms, being much less inclined to plane across the water than their British counterparts, which made them harder to spot at night, and gave them better sea-keeping qualities. Just as importantly, they used diesel engines, which used a much less volatile fuel than the petrol-powered engines in British boats. Fairmile M/Ls were too slow to catch E-Boats, while short-hulled MGBs lacked the firepower needed to destroy them. Torpedoes were no use either, as they simply passed underneath the German boats.

Clearly the Admiralty needed to develop a type of MGB that could take on these formidable opponents. Norman Hart had designed the earlier Fairmile A boats, but for this new project the Admiralty preferred to use its own man, John Holt, from the Royal Corps of Naval Constructors. His solution was to create a vessel that was capable of being mass-produced like the earlier Fairmile craft, but which was much bigger, faster and better armed than its predecessors. The hull shape he sought was essentially a combination – a bow modelled on the latest destroyers, with a stern built along more conventional Fairmile lines. Holt had actually been working on this shape of hull since the start of the war, and refined it through experiments in testing tanks until he felt he had it just right. By early 1940, he began working closely with the Fairmile staff in order to ensure the boat he designed could be prefabricated.

Propulsion was provided by four supercharged Packard engines, which thanks to the Lend-Lease Act began reaching Britain in early 1941. The hull of Holt's boat was wider than earlier Coastal Forces craft, which allowed this powerful suite of engines to be fitted ranged in two pairs in the boat's engine room. He estimated that this would provide a top speed of 31 knots, but inevitably this dropped slightly as extra weaponry was added.

The first batch of 12 MGBs was ordered in mid-March 1941. The prototype – MGB-601 – was laid down in Teddington on the River Thames in June, and she was launched just four months later. She went through extensive trials, and the Admiralty announced it was delighted with the new vessel. MGB-601 duly entered service in March 1942. By that time, another 88 boats of the class had been ordered – 28 in April 1941, and 60 more the following November, just after MGB-601 was launched. Here was real mass-production, and the ultimate proof of the Fairmile prefabrication programme. In the spring of 1941, the prefabricated parts were shipped to 16 boatyards all along the South Coast, as

This Fairmile D, MTB-724, entered service in September 1943, and was fitted with four 18in torpedo tubes. Apart from that she was no different from other 'Dog Boats'. While classed as an MTB, she – like most boats in her class – should really be regarded as a motor gun boat that happened to carry torpedoes.

MGB-605 was one of the first Fairmile D boats to enter service, being completed in June 1942. She was one of the few 'Dog Boats' that weren't fitted with scalloped torpedo recesses in her hull, but she was still reclassified as an MTB in September 1943.

well as in Scotland, North Wales and the West Country. Before the end of the year, a second batch of hulls had been sent to a further 13 British boatyards. This was going to be a truly nationwide project.

The first boats – MGBs 601–632 – were easily distinguished from later vessels because in all later craft the hull sides just forward of the bridge were scalloped out, to permit the use of torpedoes. These vessels were all turned into MTBs in September 1943 by adding two 18in torpedo tubes apiece, placed on especially high mountings so that the torpedoes could clear the boat safely when they were fired, without any risk of striking the hull. This changed role reflected a shift in the tempo of the war. Until 1942, Britain was on the defensive, in both home and Mediterranean waters. From 1943 onwards, however, the Royal Navy and its Allied counterparts were able to take the war to the enemy, following the delivery of new vessels such as the Fairmile Ds, and the advance of Allied troops in North Africa, Sicily and Italy. Where once the emphasis had been on defending British ships, now the aim was to sink those of the enemy.

The change of emphasis meant that it made sense to arm MGBs with torpedoes. At first many of these Fairmile D boats were redesignated as MGB/MTBs, but by late 1943 they were reclassified as motor torpedo boats. Of course, all that really changed was the designation – the operation of the boats remained unchanged. While the majority of Fairmile D boats were eventually armed with torpedoes, a handful remained pure MGBs until the end of the war. In general, the Fairmile D boats serving in the Mediterranean theatre tended to retain their MGB status, while those in home waters – where torpedo mounts were more readily available – were provided with the new weapon and the new designation.

The whole business of redesignation is a little confusing. MGBs 617–632, which entered service during the last three months of 1942, were all completed with two 21in torpedo tubes already fitted, and so from the outset they were classified as MGB/MTBs. Then, MGBs 633–696 were all designed with the scallops cut out of their hulls, but MGBs 641–648, 657–663 and 674 never carried torpedoes, and remained pure MGBs throughout the war. Most of these 64 boats entered service over the space of 12 months, from August 1942 onwards. Another four became MTBs 697–700 even though they lacked scalloped-out hulls, and these entered service in late 1943.

Even more vessels would follow. Another 23 Fairmile D MGBs were ordered in April 1942, while 48 more were ordered in August. A further 58 boats would follow in 1943. All of these entered service from late 1943 onwards, although some of the last vessels were not commissioned before May 1945, and the end of the war in Europe. Others were redesignated as air-sea rescue launches before they entered service. With few exceptions, all Fairmile D boats from 700 onwards were classified as MTBs rather than MGBs. MTBs 697–723 carried two 21in torpedo tubes apiece, while MTBs 724–800 were fitted with four 18in torpedo tubes, or rather they carried the fittings for them. (There is evidence that some of these tubes were never fitted.) The final batches, with pennant numbers 5001–5029, all became MTBs, and were fitted with two 21in torpedo tubes. That means that, throughout the war, a total of 229 Fairmile D boats were ordered. Of these, 48 were completed as MGBs, and only those serving in the Mediterranean retained their MGB status until the end of hostilities.

The armament of these vessels varied considerably, but the tendency was for the weaponry to increase towards the end of the conflict. The earliest vessels in the class suffered from a shortage of available weaponry, and some were fitted with older versions of the 2-pdr pom-pom, replaced by the modern powered version as supply problems eased during 1943. A much more effective weapon was the twin 20mm Oerlikon, particularly in its new powered Mark V mounting. This system gave even the early Fairmile Ds a firepower advantage over their German counterparts, and helped turn the tide of war in the narrow seas of the English Channel. In other words, they made excellent MGBs.

MGB-663, pictured off Bastia in Corsica in early 1944. She was a pure gun boat, and operated as part of the 56th MGB Flotilla, which patrolled the waters of the Tyrrhenian Sea.

MGB-658 was fitted with an American SO radar, which was an improvement over the sets issued to British Coastal Forces in the Mediterranean. In this photograph taken in March 1945, the 'Dog Boat' is pictured off Manfredonia on the Italian Adriatic coast, and is armed with a power-operated 6-pdr gun.

The messdeck of a Fairmile D – in this instance the vessel is MTB-724. While conditions were cramped, these vessels were relatively spacious compared to the shorter MGBs. The average MGB crewman was in his early 20s.

Of course, with so many Fairmile Ds in service, the vessels were used for a whole range of duties. Many remained gun boats despite their torpedo tubes, and between 1942 and 1944 they demonstrated their effectiveness over the German E-Boats. At last Coastal Forces had warships capable of defeating the enemy, and these vessels did sterling work, both in home waters and in the Mediterranean. Others were used as anti-submarine vessels, fast minelayers, navigation leaders to show the way for invasion craft, minesweepers, SOE boats, rescue launches and convoy escorts, making them even more versatile than the motor launches of the Fairmile B class.

These craft were also popular with their crews, who regarded them as 'plum appointments' within Coastal Forces. They were nicknamed 'Dog Boats' by the press, a term that was quickly adopted by their crews. They proved to be good, reliable craft, with excellent seakeeping qualities. Compared to other Coastal Forces vessels, they were comparatively dry – their long flared bow meant that their decks weren't constantly showered with spray, as was the case in other smaller MGBs. Conditions on board were cramped, but the accommodation was well laid out, with a separate wardroom amidships, a forward messdeck and petty officers' quarters in the stern.

D **FAIRMILE D 'DOG BOAT' MGB VARIANTS**

The Fairmile D class was designed to be as flexible as possible, allowing the armament of the vessels to be altered to suit the needs of a particular role or theatre. For instance, while Dog Boats serving in home waters were usually fitted with torpedo tubes (making them effectively MGB/MTBs), for the most part those serving in the Mediterranean were never armed with torpedoes. It was felt that the weight was better used in providing them with more powerful guns and besides, torpedoes were in relatively short supply.

MGB-601 (above) was the prototype of the class, and was built in Teddington on the River Thames. When she entered service in March 1942, she was armed with a 2-pdr in her bow, a twin 20mm Oerlikon in her stern, a Holman Projector amidships, two twin .5in MGs in tubs and two .303in MGs on each side of her bridge. She also carried two depth charges amidships, one on each beam. MGB-601 was sunk during an action with German E-Boats in the Dover Straits in July 1942.

MGB-624 (below) was typical of the dual-purpose MGB/MTB version of the Dog Boat. She was built in Poole in Dorset and entered service in October 1942. She was originally armed with a 2-pdr QF gun in the bow, but by late 1943 this had been replaced by an automatic 6-pdr, which is the weapon shown here. She also carried a twin 20mm Oerlikon in the stern, a Holman Projector amidships, two twin .5in MGs in tubs and two .303in MGs on each side of her bridge, as well as two 2in signal rocket launchers. Finally she carried two 21in torpedo tubes, making her a particularly well-armed and deadly little vessel.

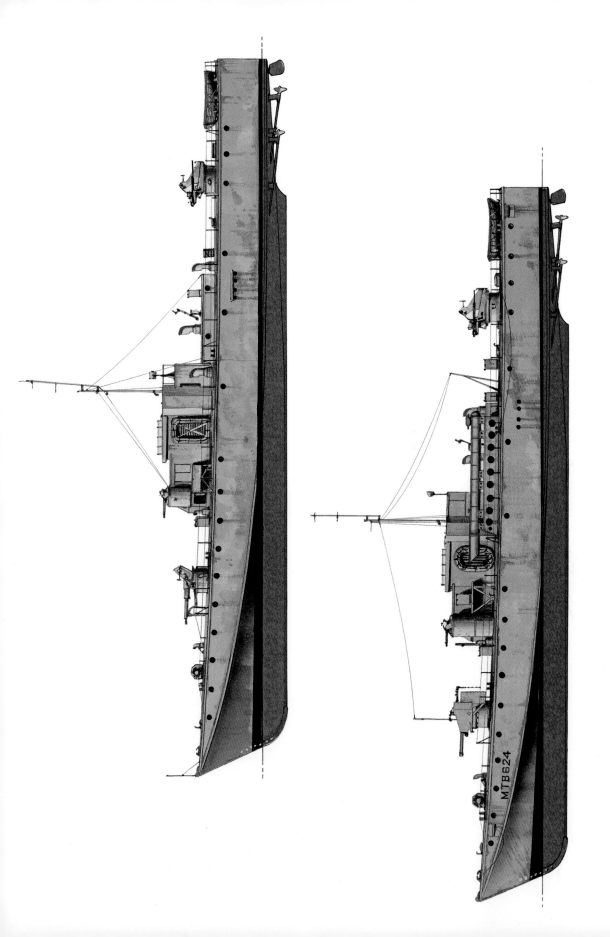

CONSTRUCTION AND WEAPONRY

Construction

The first MGBs – those produced by BPB – were real labours of love. They were built under the guidance of Hubert Scott-Paine, and his boatyard in Hove, Sussex, was capable of building boats in batches of eight to ten at a time. Not all of these were MGBs – or rather MA/SBs in their first form – as the company was also contracted to build launches, seaplane tenders and MTBs. When the war began, BPB opened up a second workshop in Holes Bay near Poole, Dorset, so it could cope with the demand. However, all these boats were built in the time-honoured way, by boat builders who followed plans, and built the vessels *in situ*.

The real achievement of the Fairmile Marine Company was to adapt this traditional form of boatbuilding for mass production. The introduction of prefabricated frames allowed their boats to be assembled in boatyards and workshops all over the world, and built by people who had no previous experience in wooden boat construction. The wooden frames were created by Fairmile in their workshops in Cobham, Surrey. These prototype pieces were then manufactured in bulk by another firm, Alfred Lockhart Ltd of Brentford, on the River Thames. Even then the actual cutting was sub-contracted to smaller companies, many of which were woodyards situated far from the sea, including companies that had made pianos or greenhouses before the war. All these prefabricated parts were then shipped to Brentford, where they were gathered together to form what was essentially a 'flat packed' little warship. The prefabricated pieces could then be shipped to the building site, and then erected to form the general shape of the boat.

The pieces were pinned in place using scrap timber, before being linked together using horizontal braces. Then the structure could be planked over – a fairly simple task, as the builders simply followed the lines of the hull. The result was that an otherwise complex boat hull could be constructed quickly, simply and in a standardized form. Other innovations included the fitting of pre-drilled steel strips, which allowed the weaponry fitted to the boats to be moved around to suit the changing needs of Coastal Forces. This is how Fairmile boats could so readily be adapted into minelayers, have torpedo tubes added or upgrade their armament.

It was a major undertaking – the delivery of parts for a Fairmile MGB involved several lorry loads, all of which had to be shipped to the builder's yard. The boat fittings were also contracted out by Fairmile, from deck cleats, rails and engine exhausts to self-sealing fuel tanks, propulsion systems and bridge fittings. All this effort was

The construction of MGB-601, the first of the Fairmile D boats, which was built in Teddington on the River Thames during 1942. Her prefabricated frames have been set in place ready for planking her hull.

coordinated by the staff at Brentford, and supervised by both Admiralty staff and the watchful experts from Fairmile. Thanks to prefabrication and mass production, at the peak of wartime production in the summer of 1943 British boatyards were able to produce more than 20 vessels a month. The whole system worked to perfection, and without it British Coastal Forces would never have had the vessels they needed to protect coastal sea lanes, or to wage their private war against the enemy's own shipping.

Propulsion

The first MGBs suffered from a multiplicity of engines. Many of the MA/SBs built by BPB immediately before the war were powered by two Napier petrol-powered engines,

Another view of MGB-601 under construction. In this photograph, the task of planking over the frames has begun. Planks were laid diagonally, to increase the strength of the hull.

which produced 1,000hp apiece. These were variants of the Napier Dagger aero engine, and gave the boats a top speed of 25 knots. The engines were less powerful and reliable than Scott-Paine had hoped, but more than adequate for the needs of the Admiralty. For foreign clients with larger budgets, Scott-Paine and BPB fitted more powerful engines – including Rolls Royce Merlin aero engines (the type of engine used in the Supermarine Spitfire aircraft) and Isotta Fraschini petrol engines from Milan. Unfortunately, both became unavailable after the outbreak of the war, as Rolls Royce concentrated on the supply of aircraft engines and the Italian engines became impossible to import.

The situation improved dramatically in April 1941, following President Roosevelt's signing of the Lend-Lease Act. This lifeline led to the supply in ever-increasing numbers of Hall-Scott engines, made in Berkeley, California, most notably the V-12 'Defender' engine, which was first produced in 1937. While these small petrol engines only produced 600hp each, they were reliable, and were fitted in most of the early Fairmile boats.

A far more successful engine was the supercharged V-12 Packard marine engine (the 4M-2500), which in its 1941 variant produced 1,350hp. By the end of the war, modifications led to 1,500hp engines being fitted in some Fairmile D boats. The 'supercharged' element referred to the use of a small air compressor to increase the oxygen available to the engine, in turn improving combustion, making the engine more powerful and more reliable. This petrol (or gasoline) engine was freshwater cooled, and weighed approximately 1.3 metric tons, which made it light enough to be replaced or repaired with relative ease.

One of the big problems with petrol-powered marine engines was noise. The sound of the hot high-pressure exhausts of un-muffled engines has been likened to the sound of balloons being burst at a rate of 600 per second. Most marine engines were cooled by freshwater, and to avoid this liquid overheating the cooling water itself had to be cooled, this time by seawater, creating a complex but necessary extra system to cram into a small engine compartment. The solution was the Dumbflow exhaust system, where a container (or 'dustbin')

E **MGB-658 FAIRMILE D MOTOR GUN BOAT**

The 'Dog Boat' was designed to counter the threat posed by German E-Boats. While slower than earlier MGBs and MTBs it was larger, and packed a far greater punch. A total of 229 of these Fairmile D MGBs were built during the war, and these were armed in a variety of ways. In general terms, the 'Dog Boats' operating in the Mediterranean were armed differently from their counterparts who served in home waters. For a start, the majority of them were never fitted with torpedo tubes, and they also seem to have been fitted with a greater variety of weaponry and equipment, including Italian quick-firing guns and American radar.

MGB-658 was built in Brixham in Devon, and entered service in April 1943. She was sent to the Mediterranean, and took part in operations in support of the landings in Sicily and the Italian mainland, before moving to a new forward base in Corsica. After the fall of Rome she and many of her fellow 'Dog Boats' were redeployed to the Adriatic, where they ended the war operating amid the islands of the Yugoslavian coast.

She was originally armed with a 40mm Oerlikon in the bow, a 6-pdr in the stern, a twin 20mm Oerlikon amidships, behind the bridge, plus two twin .5in MGs in tubs and two twin .303in Vickers MGs on each side of the bridge. By early 1945 her armament had been improved, and she was equipped as shown in the illustration. During the war MGB-658 was commanded by Lt Cornelius Burke RCN, one of several Canadian officers to command 'Dog Boats' in the Mediterranean. One of her officers – Sub Lt L.C. 'Rover' Reynolds – subsequently wrote *Motor Gunboat 658* – a spirited account of the small boat war in the Mediterranean.

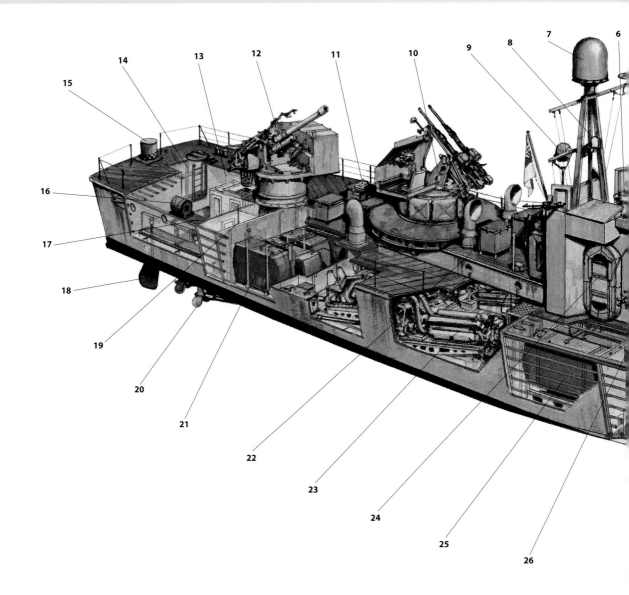

SPECIFICATIONS

Length overall: 115ft **Waterline length:** 110ft

Beam: 21ft 3in **Draught (forward):** 4ft

Displacement: 91 tons

Propulsion: Four 1,500 hp supercharged Packard engines, Ford electric engine (220 volt)

Speed: 31 knots at 2,400 rpm, 28 knots at 2,200 rpm (maximum continuous speed)

Fuel capacity and range: 5,000 gallons, 800 miles at 20 knots

Crew: 2 officers, 12 ratings (although this varied)

Armament (1945): Two automatic 6-pdr guns, two single 20mm Oerlikons, one twin 20mm Oerlikon, two twin .303in MGs, two 2in signal launchers, two depth charges.

Note: As fitted MGB-658 carried a 40mm pom-pom in place of the forward 6-pdr, and two twin .5in MGs in lieu of her two single 20mm Oerlikons.

Additional equipment: US-Built SO radar (8-mile range), radio, echo sounder, smoke generator

KEY

1. Winch
2. Automatic 6-pdr gun
3. Charthouse
4. Bridge
5. Twin .303in Vickers MG
6. Compass platform
7. American SO radar
8. Mainmast
9. Searchlight platform
10. Twin 20mm Oerlikon
11. Ammunition lockers
12. Automatic 6-pdr gun
13. Engineering (stoker's) mess
14. Tiller flat
15. Smoke apparatus
16. Depth charge (1 of 4)
17. Petty officers' mess
18. Twin rudders
19. PO's heads (stoker's heads on port side)
20. Propellers (4)
21. After fuel tanks (6)
22. Coachdeck
23. Engine room
24. Carley float (1 of 2)
25. Forward fuel tanks (6) and generator (amidships)
26. 20mm Oerlikon
27. Officer's heads and washroom (wardroom on port side)
28. Wireless and radar room
29. Commanding officer's cabin (galley on port side)
30. Forward messdeck
31. Crew's heads
32. Forepeak (store)

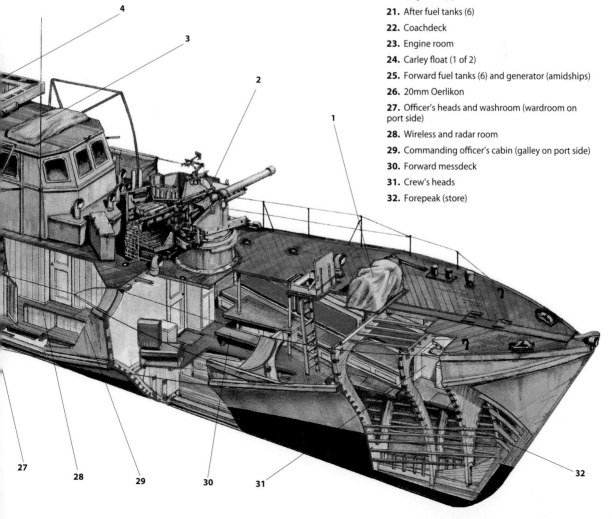

A supercharged Packard engine is lowered back into the engine room of a 'Dog Boat', after removal, repair and servicing. A Fairmile D boat was powered by four of these American-built engines, each of which generated 1,350hp.

was used to house both hot exhaust gases and water. When these had cooled, they were released through the vessel's exhausts at something close to atmospheric pressure, which meant that the exhausts murmured rather than roared. The Dumbflow system was fitted to all Fairmile D boats, which made them much quieter than their predecessors.

Armament

British MGBs existed for two main reasons – to protect other British vessels (such as coastal convoys or flotillas of vulnerable MTBs) or to engage and destroy their enemy counterparts. They also had to defend themselves against enemy aircraft, and later in the war many boats carried torpedoes, which allowed them to attack larger enemy vessels such as merchant ships or their escorts.

Because of their multi-role purpose, the MGBs carried a variety of onboard weaponry, detailed below.

Machine guns

During the opening months of the war, the majority of Coastal Forces craft were armed with nothing larger than obsolete Lewis guns, which had first been used in anger in 1914. Although these weapons were reliable, their slow rate of fire and low calibre meant that they were of very limited use, both as anti-aircraft mounts and as a means of damaging enemy E-Boats. Later, these were replaced by more modern .303in LMGs such as the Vickers gas-operated MG, which had a rate of fire of around 950 rounds per minute, compared to the Lewis' 600rpm. Both types of weapon were drum-fed. They were also easy to operate and maintain, and remained the principal light anti-aircraft weapon carried in Coastal Forces vessels until the end of the war.

An altogether more potent weapon was the .5in Vickers Mark III MG, which was usually mounted in pairs in a Mark V mounting. The weapon had a rate of fire of 700rpm, and was belt-fed from a box that held 650 rounds. A number of different mountings were used, including a pre-war Mark IV twin mount, which was cumbersome to operate. A much better system was the Mark V mounting – a small powered turret that housed a single gunner, and where ammunition was supplied in special canisters, which were easy to change in the heat of battle. The drawback was that while these .5in MGs provided an adequate anti-aircraft defence, they were still relatively ineffective against armoured German E-Boats or R-Boats.

Oerlikons

The 20mm Oerlikon gun was first developed in the 1920s by a Swiss armaments firm, and a large order of 1,500 weapons was placed by the British government immediately after the outbreak of war. However, only just over 100 weapons had been delivered to the Admiralty by the summer of 1940, when enemy E-Boats began operating from French bases. The Admiralty also had misgivings about the weapon, which had what it regarded as an unsafe breech mechanism. However, permission was granted to modify the weapons and to manufacture them under licence. A factory was established at Ruislip in Middlesex, and by the spring of 1941 these British-built 20mm Oerlikons began to enter service. By 1942, the factory was producing more than 1,000 barrels a month, and Coastal Forces vessels began to mount Oerlikons in ever-increasing numbers.

The majority of Coastal Forces MGBs were fitted with twin .5in Vickers MGs, mounted in a Mark V powered mount. While useful weapons, they lacked the punch to damage enemy E-Boats seriously, and consequently most of these mounts were replaced by 20mm Oerlikons when the larger weapons became available.

The 20mm Oerlikon was designed for close-range anti-aircraft protection, but it also proved highly effective against enemy E-Boats and other small craft. It had a rate of fire of around 475rpm, although the capacity of its cylindrical drum magazines was just 60 rounds. These were usually loaded as a mixture of ammunition types, and gunners used the catchy pneumonic 'TITS' to remember the correct order: tracer, incendiary, tracer and semi-armour piercing. Effective range was just over 1,000 yards, against both aircraft and surface targets.

Until 1942, most Oerlikons were carried on single pedestal mounts, and the earliest versions of these were unprotected by any form of gun shield. Twin mountings followed, and by late 1942 the ultimate mounting was introduced – the power-operated Mark V mount, which was fitted with twin 20mm Oerlikons. Not only did this mount offer protection for the gunners, but it was quick to traverse and ammunition supply was markedly improved. These Mark V mountings were used in late war Fairmile Cs, BMP MGBs and Fairmile Ds.

Heavy guns

The oldest gun to be carried on board Coastal Forces MGBs was the Hotchkiss 3-pdr, which first saw service during the 1880s. Large stocks dating from World War I were still held in naval stores, so it proved a useful stopgap weapon during the first year of the war, until a more effective weapon could be found to replace it. In the hands of a well-trained crew, this 1.85in hand-loaded weapon was capable of firing 15rpm and had an effective range of 3,000 yards.

The 2-pdr (40mm) gun came in several forms, the earliest of which was the Mark XI gun, on a Mark IX plinth mounting. This cannon could be used against aircraft if needed, but its primary role was to hit enemy vessels. The weapon was capable of firing high-explosive (HE) rounds, and had an effective range of 1,500 yards. It was hand-loaded, which meant that its rate of fire was similar to the Hotchkiss. The Rolls Royce 2-pdr was introduced in mid-1940; although an improvement on the existing hand-loaded 2-pdr as it was faster

to use, it was awkward to operate, but it had a slightly higher rate of fire. These early guns were replaced when 'pom-pom' versions or Oerlikons became available.

A much more satisfactory weapon was the 2-pdr Vickers 'pom-pom', which resembled an over-sized Vickers MG. The weapon was first introduced into service in 1915, but it proved both reliable and effective, although when combined with its Mark II mount it was too heavy for most small MGBs to carry. The weapon was belt-fed, and had a rate of fire of around 200rpm, although the belt itself only carried 25 rounds. It was carried in the Fairmile C MGB.

The 2-pdr came into its own when the 'pom-pom' was improved, and fitted to a power-operated mount similar to that described for the

A single 20mm Oerlikon, mounted in the stern of a 70ft BPB MGB. Later in the war, two-barrelled mounts became more common and by 1944 most Oerlikons were fitted onto powered mounts. Note the safety bar, to prevent the gunner hitting the boat's superstructure.

Oerlikon. In this form the semi-automatic weapon had a rate of fire of 98rpm, which was fed in belts of 14 rounds each, and stored in trays that held eight belts, allowing just over a minute of continuous fire without reloading. The effective range of this power-mounted Mark XII 'pom-pom' was a respectable 3,000 yards.

Towards the end of 1944, a power-mounted 6-pdr entered service, and was carried in a range of Coastal Forces MGBs and MTBs. It was based on a British anti-tank gun, but mounted on a Mark VII power-operated turret, fitted with a Molins auto-loading system. This powerful weapon was more than a match for most German E-Boats, and had a rate of fire of 40rpm, with an effective range out to 6,000 yards.

Other weapons

While many MGBs and SGBs carried torpedoes, these weapons are covered in detail in the Osprey companion volume to this publication, *British Motor Torpedo Boat, 1939–45*. Suffice to say that both 18in and 21in torpedoes were carried, depending on vessel type and availability. Similarly, mines and depth charges were used too, but although the latter weapon was sometimes used offensively during Coastal Forces actions, neither was really a main form of offensive weapon.

Another widely used weapon was the Holman Projector, an anti-aircraft device that used compressed air to fire a hand-grenade up to a height of around 600ft. The weapon had a rate of fire of approximately 20rpm. While these were spectacularly ineffective, they did tend to surprise oncoming aircraft, as the large puff produced by the exploding hand grenade looked like bursting flak, fired by a much larger and deadlier weapon. Another strange weapon was the 2in rocket-projected signal flare, which was essentially used to fire starshells. These resembled MGs, and were usually mounted on either side of the hull, immediately forward of the bridge, in a variety of British MGBs.

Finally, all Coastal Forces vessels carried smoke floats or smoke-making apparatus. Smoke floats were thrown over the side, and burned for up to ten minutes. The chloro-sulphonic acid (CSA) smoke-producing apparatus was usually mounted in the stern of an MGB, and came in a range of forms. For the most part, these could be used to produce a dense white smoke screen, which would also last for about ten minutes, depending of course on wind strength.

MGBS IN ACTION

In a book of this size there is all too little space to describe fully how these boats and their weaponry operated in action. The Bibliography contains a number of excellent books that provide vivid accounts of MGB actions, written by those who took part in them. The following brief accounts of actions, however, give a flavour of what it was like to go into battle at 30 knots, sitting on top of a petrol tank, protected from enemy tracer by a thin layer of plywood.

In March 1941, a patrol of BPB MGBs left Felixstowe, in a failed attempt to intercept an enemy convoy. The action began on their way home, as recounted by Sub Lt Leaf RNVR, of the 6th MGB Flotilla:

A Rolls Royce 2-pdr mounted in the stern of a Fairmile C MGB. While less formidable than other 2-pdr (40mm) guns, this hand-loaded weapon was widely used in MGBs until replaced by more powerful weapons.

An automatic 6-pdr QF gun on a power-operated Mk VII mounting. These guns were added to some of the late war 'Dog Boats', giving them an impressive level of firepower. The Molins auto-loader held seven rounds, but had to be reloaded by hand.

Daybreak found us passing close to Brown Ridge Buoy. It was light enough to see two or three miles when we altered course for home and breakfast after a long night of waiting. Imagine our surprise at this late hour when we saw a German E-Boat approaching on a converging course on the starboard bow. He came nearer and opened fire with a long crackly burst as he crossed our bow about 75 yards ahead. We then shot him up from astern and turned to run alongside him. His tracers were fascinating. You could see them coming in little groups of eight to ten, mostly low overhead. One or two hit us and exploded. After a quarter of an hour a second E-Boat came up astern. We turned to port to depth charge her, but got caught with cross-fire instead, and the first E-Boat escaped. As we were only about 20 miles from Holland and on fire in the after compartment, we broke off and made back home – none the more victorious.

A more successful encounter took place on 13–14 March 1942, when three 70ft Elco MGBs of the 7th MGB Flotilla left Lowestoft to hunt for the enemy off the Dutch coast. The night patrol was uneventful, but as dawn broke an E-Boat emerged out of the mist, and what followed is described by the skipper of MGB-87:

She came on serenely enough, only ten miles from home and looking forward to a day's rest after her night's misdemeanours; but the Germans had another surprise coming to them as they saw three white ensigns fluttering in the breeze... she swerved to port and our boats followed, giving tongue with their roaring exhausts. Every twist and turn was headed off as she tried to run for home, but she was finally kept on a course which was none of her choosing. We had the legs of her and we slowly crept up, although she was doing 40 knots; and all the while we were giving her everything we'd got; bits were flying off her in all directions and a burst from one of her cannons stopped as abruptly as it had begun. Captains, First Lieutenants and Coxwains all found time to empty a few personal [ammunition] pans. The Coxwain of [MGB] 88 particularly distinguished himself by emptying his revolver at his opposite number in the wheelhouse of the E-Boat.

Some of the crew jumped overboard and others scrambled on deck with their hands up. At last we could throw down our engines which had been running for a good half-hour flat out. Mr. Packard might well rise from his grave and take a bow – not to mention the maintenance people ashore. We closed and prepared to board while [MGBs] 88 and 91 started picking up survivors.

The enemy – a battered German E-Boat (S-111) captured during a surface action off the Dutch coast in March 1942. She is shown flying the British white ensign – her Kriegsmarine (German Navy) flag has already been taken as a souvenir.

A group of 70ft BPB MGBs leaving harbour at the start of a patrol during the early summer of 1942. Cross-channel sweeps of this kind were virtually a nightly occurrence throughout the war.

The damaged E-Boat (pictured on page 34) was taken in tow, with a white ensign flying from a jury-rigged mast. Unfortunately, another group of E-Boats was encountered on the voyage home, and the prize had to be scuttled. However, MGB-87 still had her German prisoners, and entered Felixstowe in triumph, with the German flag flying beneath her white ensign.

VESSEL LISTINGS

M/L and MGB Specifications

60ft British Power Boat MGB

Numbers: MGBs 1–5, 22–39, 40–45, 49
Dimensions: Length: 60ft 3in; Beam: 13ft 3in
Draught: 2ft 9in
Displacement: 19 tons
Propulsion: Two Napier engines (MGBs 40–45 had Rolls Royce Merlin engines)
Speed: 25 knots (40 knots for MGBs 40–45)

British warships and amphibious craft on their way to Dieppe, during the disastrous raid on the French port in 1942. The Fairmile C boat MGB-321 can be seen in the foreground.

This rare photograph shows a briefing of Coastal Forces commanders during operations in support of the Normandy landings in June 1944. The officer addressing the other officers is Lt Cdr Peter Scott, RNVR (Royal Navy Volunteer Reserve).

Armament (as designed): One twin .303in Lewis LMG later replaced with two quad .303in LMGs in powered turrets, one on each side of the bridge. MGBs 40–45 were armed with one 2-pdr 'pom-pom' aft, and two twin .5in MGs in powered turrets
Complement: 1 officer, 8 ratings (2 officers on MGBs 40–45)

Note: Originally, MGBs 1–39 began as MA/SBs, but were converted into MGBs in 1940. MGBs 40–45 were built by BPB as MTBs for the Royal Netherlands Navy, but they escaped to Britain in 1940 and were commissioned as Royal Navy MGBs. In 1941–42, MGBs 1–2, 4–5, 22–39 and 49 were converted into air-sea rescue launches. MGBs 44–45 were transferred to the Polish Navy in 1944.

MGB-314 DURING THE ST NAZAIRE RAID, MARCH 1942

The raid on the French port of St Nazaire in March 1942 was one of the most daring commando operations of the war. The port lay at the mouth of the River Loire, and contained the only dry dock on the French Atlantic seaboard large enough to take the German battleship *Tirpitz*. The aim of the raid was the destruction of the dry dock, which was achieved by packing the obsolete lend-lease destroyer HMS *Campbeltown* with explosives and ramming the dock gates with it. A specially converted MTB (MTB-74) would also destroy the Old Entrance gates, used by German U-Boats. Meanwhile, the commandos led by Lt Col Newman would destroy what they could of the port facilities.

The commandos were embarked on a flotilla of 15 Fairmile B M/Ls, three of which were fitted with torpedoes to use on any German shipping they encountered. Newman and his headquarters party were carried on board Lt Curtis' Fairmile C vessel, MGB-314. Shortly after the *Campbeltown* rammed the dock gates, MGB-314 landed Newman near the Old Entrance, coming under heavy fire from German flak guns as she did so. This scene shows the boat approaching the southern side of the Old Entrance, while the *Campbeltown* can be seen in the background, lodged firmly on top of the gates of the Normandie Dock. Out in the river itself ML-268 is ablaze, having been hit repeatedly by German guns. MGB-314 was so badly damaged during the attack and its immediate aftermath that she had to be scuttled in the estuary of the River Loire.

70ft British Power Boat MGB

Numbers: MGBs 6–21, 46, 50–67

Dimensions: Length: 70ft; Beam: 20ft

Draught: 4ft

Displacement: 31 tons (MGB-46: 32 tons, MGBs 50–67: 34 tons)

Propulsion: Two Napier engines (MGB-46 had three Rolls Royce Merlin engines, MGBs 50–67 had three Isotta-Fraschini engines)

Speed: 23 knots (40 knots for MGBs 46, 50–67)

Armament (as designed): One Rolls Royce 2-pdr or one single 20mm Oerlikon aft; two twin .5in MGs, in powered turrets on each side of bridge; one single .5in MG in powered turret amidships (behind bridge). MGB-46 did not carry the single MG. MGBs 50–67 were armed with one single 20m Oerlikon or one quad .303in LMG aft, two twin .5in MGs in powered turrets on either side of the bridge and two twin .303in LMGs on each beam

Complement: 2 officers, 8 ratings (1 less officer on MGB-46, two more ratings on MGBs 50–67).

Note: MGB 46 was built by BPB for the Royal Netherlands Navy as an MTB, but escaped to Britain in 1940 and was commissioned as a Royal Navy MGB. MGBs 50–67 were built by BPB for the French Navy as MA/SBs, but were completed as Royal Navy MGBs.

71ft 9in British Power Boat MGB

Numbers: MGBs 74–81, 107–176

Dimensions: Length: 71ft 9in; Beam: 20ft 7in

Draught: 5ft 9in

Displacement: 51½ tons

Propulsion: Three supercharged Packard engines

Speed: 42 knots

Armament (as designed): One 2-pdr 'pom-pom' forward; one single 20mm Oerlikon aft; two twin .303in Lewis LMGs on each side of bridge; one Holman Projector amidships, two depth charges amidships

Complement: 2 officers, 10 ratings

70ft Higgins MGB

Numbers: MGBs 69–73, 100–106

Dimensions: Length: 70ft; Beam: 19ft 9in

Draught: 4ft

Displacement: 40 tons

Propulsion: Three supercharged Packard engines

Speed: 40 knots

Armament (varied): Usually one single 20mm Oerlikon aft; two twin .5in MGs on each side of bridge

Complement: 2 officers, 7 ratings

Note: MGBs 68–73 and 100–106 were built in America for the Finnish Navy, but transferred to Britain instead.

MGB-10, a 70ft BPB MGB, pictured in Dover Harbour in early 1942. This pre-war MA/SB was still lightly armed, with a Rolls Royce 2-pdr aft and – unusually in her class – a single MG turret, mounted on her centreline, abaft the bridge. Later that year this was replaced by two twin MGs, mounted in turrets on either side of the bridge. Note the two smoke floats, carried on her stern.

78ft Higgins MGB

Numbers: MGBs 177–192
Dimensions: Length: 78ft 6in; Beam: 20ft 1in
Draught: 5ft 3in
Displacement: 43 tons
Propulsion: Three supercharged Packard engines
Speed: 40 knots
Armament (when received): One single 20mm Oerlikon aft; two twin .5in
    MGs on each side of bridge; two depth charges amidships
Complement: 2 officers, 9 ratings

MGB-46, a 70ft BPB vessel. She was 'stolen' by the Dutch and served as TMB-51 until she returned to Britain when Holland was overrun in May 1940.

Note: These vessels were built for the US Navy, and transferred into Royal Naval service as part of the Lend-Lease programme.

70ft Elco MGB

Numbers: MGBs 82–93
Dimensions: Length: 70ft; Beam: 19ft 11in
Draught: 4ft 6in
Displacement: 32 tons
Propulsion: Three supercharged Packard engines
Speed: 42 knots
Armament (when received): Two twin .5in MGs in powered Dewandre
    turrets on each side of bridge; two depth charges amidships
Complement: 2 officers, 8 ratings

Note: These vessels were built for the US Navy as PTCs 1–12, and transferred into Royal Navy service as part of the Lend-Lease programme.

117ft Camper & Nicholson MGB

Numbers: MGBs 502–509
Dimensions: Length: 117ft; Beam: 20ft 3in
Draught: 4ft 4in
Displacement: 95 tons
Propulsion: Three Davey Paxman diesel engines (MGB-509 was fitted with
    three supercharged Packard engines)
Speed: 28 knots (MGB-509: 31 knots)

A rare picture of a Camper & Nicholson 117ft boat – MGB-509 – pictured after the war, by which time her armament had been removed and her pennant number changed to MTB-2009. These vessels were originally built for Turkish naval service, until requisitioned by the Admiralty in late 1943.

Armament (as designed): One 2-pdr 'pom-pom' aft; two twin .5in MGs in powered turrets on each side of bridge; two twin .303in LMGs on each side of the bridge; one Holman Projector, two 21in torpedo tubes; 12 depth charges amidships. These vessels were rearmed in early 1945 with the 2-pdr 'pom-pom' moved to the bow, a single twin 20mm Oerlikon in a powered mount amidships and a 6-pdr QF aft. The vessels retained their other weaponry, although only four depth charges were carried.

Complement: 3 officers, 18 ratings

Note: these vessels were ordered by the Turkish Navy, but were taken over by the Royal Navy in February 1941, before they were completed. Only MGB-502, MGB-503 and MGB-509 were initially completed as MGBs – the rest were turned into blockade runners, designed to carry cargos of Swedish ball bearings through the Skaggerak. They were also given names; HMS *Hopewell* (MGB-504), HMS *Nonsuch* (MGB-505), HMS *Gay Viking* (MGB-506), HMS *Gay Corsair* (MGB-507) and HMS *Master Standfast* (MGB-508). As blockade runners, their armament was reduced to the single twin 20mm Oerlikon amidships, and two twin Lewis LMGs. In September 1944, the surviving blockade runners reverted to being MGBs, and were re-equipped and renumbered as such. Also note that with the rearmament in early 1945 the vessels were also renumbered by adding 1,500 to their pennant numbers (e.g. MGB-504 became MGB 2004).

117ft Camper & Nicholson MGB (modified)
Numbers: MGBs 511–518
Dimensions: Length: 117ft; Beam: 22ft 3in
Draught: 4ft 4in
Displacement: 115 tons
Propulsion: Three supercharged Packard engines
Speed: 31 knots
Armament (as designed): Two automatic 6-pdrs in power turret (one each in bow and stern); two single 20mm Oerlikons on each side of the bridge; four 18in torpedo tubes; two 2in rocket flare projectors; two depth charges
Complement: 3 officers, 27 ratings

Note: These vessels were designed as improved versions of the original 117ft MGBs, intended to be better sea boats. Unlike their predecessors, they were also built exclusively for Royal Navy service. They were armed with a powerful torpedo armament, so technically they were MGB/MTBs. However, for operational purposes they retained their MGB nomenclature.

Fairmile A M/L
Numbers: M/Ls 100–111
Dimensions: Length: 110ft; Beam: 17ft 5in
Draught: 6ft 6in
Displacement: 60 tons

Propulsion: Three Hall-Scott Defender
    engines
Speed: 25 knots
Armament (as escort): One Hotchkiss
    3-pdr aft; two single .303in
    Lewis MGs on pedestals in bow;
    12 depth charges
Complement: 2 officers, 14 ratings

Note: When these vessels were
rearmed as minesweepers, in early
1942, the 3-pdr was moved to the
bow, one twin 20mm Oerlikon was
mounted aft and one single 20mm
Oerlikon was mounted amidships, after the funnel was removed to make way
for this extra armament amidships. The depth charges were replaced by a
cargo of either nine moored mines or six ground mines.

The crews of two BPB MGBs
display the German
Kriegsmarine flag, captured
from an enemy trawler during a
surface action, 1942. The small
size of these crews meant that
boats and flotillas formed
tight-knit communities.

Fairmile B M/L

Numbers: MLs 112–311, 336–500, 511–600, 801–933, 4001–4004
Dimensions: Length: 112ft; Beam: 18ft 3in
Draught: 4ft 9in
Displacement: 65 tons
Propulsion: Two Hall-Scott Defender engines
Speed: 20 knots
Armament (as escort): One Hotchkiss 3-pdr aft; two single .303in Lewis
    MGs on pedestals; 12 depth charges; (as MA/SW vessel): One Hotchkiss
    3-pdr in bow; one single 20mm Oerlikon amidships; one Holman
    Projector amidships; one twin 20mm Oerlikon aft; two twin .303in Lewis
    LMGs on pedestals; 14 depth charges, with 'Y' launcher; (as minelayer):
    One Hotchkiss 3-pdr in bow; one single 20mm Oerlikon amidships; one
    twin 20mm Oerlikon aft; two twin .303in Lewis LMGs on sides of bridge;
    nine moored mines or six ground mines
Complement: 2 officers, 14 ratings

Note: This vessel was the workhorse of Coastal Forces, and its role and
armament varied considerably. The armament listed above could vary
considerably, depending on role, theatre of operations or availability of
weaponry. In early 1941, approximately 50 of these vessels were equipped
with two 21in torpedo tubes, taken from obsolete Lend-Lease destroyers.
When the threat of invasion passed in mid 1941, these were removed.
MA/SW vessels were fitted with Asdic. In early 1944, all remaining Holman
Projectors were landed, and two single 2in rocket signal guns were fitted on
pedestal mounts forward of the bridge.

Fairmile C MGB

Numbers: MGBs 312–335
Dimensions: Length: 71ft 9in; Beam: 20ft 7in
Draught: 5ft 9in
Displacement: 51½ tons
Propulsion: Three supercharged Hall-Scott Defender engines
Speed: 26½ knots

HMS *Grey Goose* (SGB-9) entering harbour. These Denny Steam Gun Boats were reinforced with armoured plate during the war, and their armament was gradually increased, making them formidable E-Boat hunters.

Armament (as designed): Two single 2-pdr 'pom-poms' (one in bow in power turret, one aft); two twin .5in MG in power turrets amidships; two twin .303in Lewis LMGs on sides of bridge
Complement: 2 officers, 10 ratings

Note: By mid 1943 these vessels were rearmed with 2-pdr power turrets both fore and aft, and two twin 20mm Oerlikons replaced the MGs in the power turrets amidships. A single twin 20mm Oerlikon was also mounted amidships.

Denny SGB
Numbers: SGB 3–9
Dimensions: Length: 145ft 8in; Beam: 20ft
Draught: 5ft 6in
Displacement: 175 tons
Propulsion: Two Metropolitan-Vickers steam turbines
Speed: 35 knots
Armament (as designed): Two single 6-pdr guns in powered turrets (one each in bow and stern); one 3-pdr amidships; two twin 20mm Oerlikons in powered turrets on either side of bridge; two 21in torpedo tubes
Complement: 3 officers, 24 ratings (later increased to 31 ratings)

AB (Able Seaman) With and Signalman Clegg, two members of the ship's company of the Denny Steam Gun Boat *Grey Shark* (SGB-6), photographed in the spring of 1943. Apart from the commanding officers, most men serving in Coastal Forces were below the age of 25.

Note: SGB-1 and SGB-2 were cancelled before they entered service. With the exception of SGB-7, which was sunk days earlier, the rest were all given names in June 1942; *Grey Seal* (SGB-3), *Grey Fox* (SGB-4), *Grey Owl* (SGB-5), *Grey Shark* (SGB-6), *Grey Wolf* (SGB-8) and *Grey Goose* (SGB-9). In mid 1944, these vessels were all converted into fast minesweepers, during the preparations for the Normandy landings.

Fairmile D 'Dog Boat' MGB
Numbers: MGB 601–663, and 674. Of these, 601–640 and 649–646 were later converted into MTBs. Fairmile D boats 664–673, 675–800 and 5001–5029 were all classified from the start as MTBs.
Dimensions: Length: 115ft; Beam: 21ft 3in
Draught: 5ft 1in

Displacement: 91 tons (105 tons when fitted with torpedoes)
Propulsion: Four supercharged Packard engines
Speed: 31 knots
Armament (as designed): One single 2-pdr 'pom-pom' in power turret in bow; two twin .5in MGs in power turrets amidships; one Holman Projector amidships; one twin 20mm Oerlikon in power turret aft; two twin .303in LMGs on sides of bridge; two depth charges
Complement: 2 officers, 12 ratings

The crew of the Fairmile D boat MGB-658, photographed in Malta in March 1945. The original complement of a 'Dog Boat' was two officers and 12 ratings, but due to extra weaponry this number had doubled by the end of the war.

Note: Many of these vessels were additionally fitted with two 21in torpedo tubes. The first boats of the series were built as pure MGBs, but later vessels had their gunwales modified to permit the firing of torpedoes. From MGB-724 onwards these vessels were fitted with four 18in torpedo tubes as standard. The remaining weaponry of these vessels was designed to be flexible, and while most vessels entered service with a fairly standard suite of weapons, these were soon modified, replaced or upgraded. In fact, the weaponry varied considerably, depending on role, theatre and availability. MGBs 602–616, 664, 673, 675–680 were reclassified as MTBs in September 1943, and were to become MTBs 499–521, but it appears they ended up retaining their pennant numbers. MGBs 649–656, 664–673, 675–723 were reclassified as MTBs at the same time, but retained their pennant numbers. MGBs 641–648, 657–663 and 674 were never reclassified, remaining MGBs throughout the war.

MGB and SGB Losses

MGB-12 (70ft BPB) – Sunk by mine off Milford Haven, 3 February 1941
MGB-17 (70ft BPB) – Sunk by mine off Normandy beaches, 11 June 1944
MGB-18 (70ft BPB) – Sunk during surface action off Terschelling, Holland, 30 September 1942
MGB-19 (70ft BPB) – Destroyed by bombing on slipway, Portsmouth, 6 November 1942
MGB-62 (70ft BPB) – Sunk in collision, North Sea, 9 August 1941
MGB-64 (70ft BPB) – Foundered during storm in English Channel, 8 August 1943
MGB-76 (71ft 9in BPB) – Sunk during surface action, North Sea, 6 October 1942
MGB-78 (71ft 9in BPB) – Beached and destroyed during surface action, Dutch coast, 3 October 1942
MGB-79 (71ft 9in BPB) – Sunk during surface action off Hook of Holland, 28 February 1943
MGB-90 (70ft Elco) – Destroyed by fire, Portland Harbour, 6 July 1941
MGB-92 (70ft Elco) – Destroyed by fire, Portland Harbour, 6 July 1941
MGB-98 (French MGB) – Destroyed during air raid, Gosport, June 1941
MGB-99 (French MGB) – Constructive loss, April 1945

MGB-109 (71ft 9in BPB) – Badly damaged by mine, 7 February 1943; decommissioned two weeks later

MGB-110 (71ft 9in BPB) – Sunk during surface action off Dunkirk, 29 May 1943

MGB-313 (Fairmile C) – Sunk by mine off Normandy beaches, 16 August 1944

MGB-314 (Fairmile C) – Badly damaged and scuttled off St Nazaire, 28 March 1942

MGB-326 (Fairmile C) – Sunk by mine off Normandy beaches, 28 June 1944

MGB-328 (Fairmile C) – Sunk during attack on enemy convoy, Dover Straits, 21 July 1942

MGB-335 (Fairmile C) – Badly damaged and scuttled during surface action in North Sea, 11 September 1942

MGB-501 (Camper & Nicholson experimental) – Destroyed by accidental explosion off Land's End, 27 July 1942

MGB-601 (Fairmile D) – Sunk during surface action, Dover Straits, 24 July 1942

MGB-622 (Fairmile D) – Sunk during surface action off Terschelling, Holland, 10 March 1943

MGB-631 (Fairmile D) – Transferred to Royal Norwegian Navy, August 1942. Ran aground on Norwegian coast and captured, 14 March 1943

MGB-635 (Fairmile D) – Badly damaged, and subsequently sunk as a target off Malta, July 1945

MGB-641 (Fairmile D) – Sunk by shore battery, Straits of Messina, 15 July 1943

MGB-644 (Fairmile D) – Damaged by mine and scuttled off Marsala, Sicily, 26 June 1943

MGB-648 (Fairmile D) – Sunk by enemy aircraft, Pantellerea, Straits of Sicily, 14 June 1943

MGB-663 (Fairmile D) – Sunk by mine off Po Estuary, 10 October 1944

MGB-2002 (formerly Camper & Nicholson MGB-502) – Sunk by mine in Skagerrak, 12 May 1945

MGB-2007 (formerly Camper & Nicholson MGB-507 – *Gay Corsair*) – Ran aground and foundered off Aberdeen, 24 May 1945

SGB-7 (Denny) – Sunk during surface action in Dover Straits, 19 June 1942

G   **MGB-655 DURING A CONVOY BATTLE NEAR GIGLIO, ITALY, JANUARY 1944**

By the start of 1944, British and American MGBs and MTBs were based in Corsica, where they were able to interdict German coastal traffic in the Tyrrhenian Sea. They tended to operate together, allowing the British 'Dog Boat' commanders to take advantage of the better radar equipment issued to the American PT Boats. This scene shows an action that took place off the Tuscan coast, near the island of Giglio, between Dog Boats of the 56th MGB Flotilla and a well-armed German coastal convoy consisting of F-Lighters and E-Boats.

Thanks to their radar, the British approached unseen, coming up astern of the convoy. They attacked in line astern, with MGB-657 leading, followed by MGB-658, MGB-663, MGB-659 and finally MGB-655. In this view of the engagement, the British have just opened fire on one of the F-Lighters, which is now blazing fiercely. The British found that because the German gunners were so well protected by concrete-reinforced emplacements, they tended to shelter during an engagement, rather than return the British fire. The exposed British gunners had no option but to rely on their firepower.

The E-Boats were more of a threat, and in this engagement one even tried to ram MGB-655, which is pictured in the foreground, bringing up the rear of the British line. Incidentally, of all the Dog Boats in the flotilla, MGB-655 was the only vessel armed with torpedoes.

MGBs listed by Pennant Number

Pennant Number	MGB Type	Commissioned	Notes
1–5	60ft BPB	MA/SBs 1938–39, MGBs from June 1940	
6–21	70ft BPB	MA/SBs 1939, MGBs from October 1940	
22–39	60ft BPB	MA/SB 1939, MGBs from June 1940	
40–45	60ft BPB	June 1940	Built for the Dutch, Norwegian and Swedish navies, then requisitioned
46	70ft BPB	July 1940	Built for the Dutch Navy as TMB-51 and commissioned after its escape from Holland
47–48	75ft White	October 1940	Built for the Polish Navy and requisitioned. MGB-48 became the Polish S-1
49	60ft White	June 1940	Formerly the *Bulldog*, of the India Store Department
50–67	70ft BPB	December 1940–February 1941	Built for the French Navy as VTB-23–40, and requisitioned
68	81ft Higgins	April 1941	Lend-Lease – formerly PT-6
69–73	70ft Higgins	September 1941	Lend-Lease - Built for the Finnish Navy and requisitioned
74–81	71ft 9in BPB	May 1942–January 1943	
82–93	70ft Elco	April 1941	Lend-Lease – formerly PTC 1–12
94–97	Not used		
98–99	65ft 7in AC de la Loire	June 1940	Built for the French Navy as VTB-11 and VTB-12 and requisitioned
100–106	70ft Higgins	October 1941	Lend-Lease – built for the Finnish Navy and requisitioned
107–176	71ft 9in BPB	September 1942–January 1945	
177–192	78ft Higgins	October 1944	Transfer of US 15th MTB Flotilla
193–311	Not used		
312–335	Fairmile C	June–October 1941	
336–500	Not used		
501	110ft Camper & Nicholson	May 1942	Experimental prototype of MGBs 502–509 and 511–518
502–509	117ft Camper & Nicholson	August–September 1941	Built for the Turkish Navy and requisitioned
510	73ft Vosper	1943	Experimental MGB version of the 73ft Vosper MTB design
511–518	117ft Camper & Nicholson	1944	MGB/MTB – many were redesignated as MTBs
519–600	Not used		
601–800	Fairmile D	March 1942–July 1945	MGB/MTB
801–2000	Not used		
2001	Fairmile F	September 1943	Experimental
2002–5000	Not used		
5001–5029	Fairmile D	December 1944–July 1945	MGB/MTB
SGB 3–9	Denny	February–July 1942	SGB-1 and SGB-2 were cancelled before completion

BIBLIOGRAPHY

Barnett, Corelli, *Engage the Enemy More Closely: The Royal Navy in the Second World War* (London, Penguin, 1991)

Cooper, Bryan, *The E-Boat Threat* (London, Macdonald and Jane's, 1970)

Gardiner, Robert (ed.), *Conway's All the World's Fighting Ships, 1922–1946* (London and Annapolis, MD, Conway Maritime Press, 1980)

Hitchens, Antony, *Gunboat Command: the Biography of Lt. Cdr. Robert Hichens DSO DSC RNVR* (Barnsley, Pen & Sword, 2007)

Jefferson, David, *Coastal Forces at War: Royal Navy 'Little Ships' in World War 2* (London, Patrick Stephens, 1996)

Kemp, Paul J., *British Coastal Forces of World War II* (London, ISO Publications, 1997)

Lambert, John, *Fairmile 'D' Motor Torpedo Boat* (London, Conway Maritime Press, 2005)

Lambert, John and Ross, A.I., *Allied Coastal Forces of World War II: Volume I: Fairmile Designs and US Sub Chasers* (London, Conway Maritime Press, 1990)

Lambert, John and Ross, A.I., *Allied Coastal Forces of World War II: Volume II: Vosper MTBs and US Elcos* (London, Conway Maritime Press, 1993)

North, A.J.D., *Royal Naval Coastal Forces, 1939–1945* (London, Almark Publications 1972)

Polmar, Norman and Morison, Samuel L., *PT Boats at War: World War II to Vietnam* (Osceola WI, MBI Publishing, 1999)

Reynolds, Leonard C., *Motor Gunboat 658: the Small Boat War in the Mediterranean* (London, William Kimber, 1955, reprinted by Cassell, 2002)

Reynolds, Leonard C., *Home Waters MTBs and MGBs at War* (Stroud, Sutton, 2000)

Reynolds, Leonard C., *Dog Boats at War: Royal Navy D Class MTBs and MGBs, 1939–1945* (Stroud, Sutton, 1998)

Lt Cdr Robert Hichens RNVR developed MGB tactics during the early part of the war. This photograph shows him briefing the officers of the 18th MGB Flotilla before a patrol. Hichens was killed in action in April 1943.

INDEX

Note; letters in **bold** refer to plates and illustrations.